EXPLORING COUNTRIES

Iran

by Walter Simmons

BLASTOFF! READERS

5

BELLWETHER MEDIA • MINNEAPOLIS, MN

JUL 0 6 2011

Note to Librarians, Teachers, and Parents:

Blastoff! Readers are carefully developed by literacy experts and combine standards-based content with developmentally appropriate text.

Level 1 provides the most support through repetition of high-frequency words, light text, predictable sentence patterns, and strong visual support.

Level 2 offers early readers a bit more challenge through varied simple sentences, increased text load, and less repetition of high-frequency words.

Level 3 advances early-fluent readers toward fluency through increased text and concept load, less reliance on visuals, longer sentences, and more literary language.

Level 4 builds reading stamina by providing more text per page, increased use of punctuation, greater variation in sentence patterns, and increasingly challenging vocabulary.

Level 5 encourages children to move from "learning to read" to "reading to learn" by providing even more text, varied writing styles, and less familiar topics.

Whichever book is right for your reader, Blastoff! Readers are the perfect books to build confidence and encourage a love of reading that will last a lifetime!

This edition first published in 2011 by Bellwether Media, Inc.

No part of this publication may be reproduced in whole or in part without written permission of the publisher. For information regarding permission, write to Bellwether Media, Inc., Attention: Permissions Department, . 5357 Penn Avenue South, Minneapolis, MN 55419.

Library of Congress Cataloging-in-Publication Data
Simmons, Walter (Walter G.)
 Iran / by Walter Simmons.
    p. cm. – (Exploring countries) (Blastoff! readers)
 Includes bibliographical references and index.
 Summary: "Developed by literacy experts for students in grades three through seven, this book introduces young readers to the geography and culture of Iran"–Provided by publisher.
 ISBN 978-1-60014-591-9 (hardcover : alk. paper)
 1. Iran–Juvenile literature. I. Title.
 DS254.75.S46 2011
 955–dc22   2010039203

Text copyright © 2011 by Bellwether Media, Inc. BLASTOFF! READERS and associated logos are trademarks and/or registered trademarks of Bellwether Media, Inc.

Printed in the United States of America, North Mankato, MN.

010111   1176

Contents

Where Is Iran?	4
The Land	6
Lake Urmia	8
Wildlife	10
The People	12
Daily Life	14
Going to School	16
Working	18
Playing	20
Food	22
Holidays	24
Persepolis	26
Fast Facts	28
Glossary	30
To Learn More	31
Index	32

Armenia

Azerbaijan

Turkmenistan

Turkey

Caspian Sea

Iraq

Tehran
⭐

Iran

Persian Gulf

Did you know?

Over 2,000 years ago, Iran was the center of the Persian Empire. This empire ruled over parts of Africa, Asia, and Europe.

Afghanistan

Pakistan

Iran is a country in the **Middle East** that covers 636,372 square miles (1,648,195 square kilometers). Seven countries border it. To the west lies the nation of Iraq. Pakistan and Afghanistan are Iran's eastern neighbors. A long northern border touches Turkmenistan, Azerbaijan, Armenia, and Turkey. The Persian **Gulf** and the Gulf of Oman wash onto the country's southern coast. The Caspian Sea sits to the north of Iran's capital, Tehran.

Gulf of Oman

Mount Damavand

Iran is a land of mountains, plains, deserts, and forests. The Zagros Mountains form a long chain in western Iran. Mount Damavand, the nation's tallest mountain, is a **dormant** volcano. It rises more than 18,400 feet (5,600 meters) in the Alborz Mountains, a steep range in the north. Many mountainsides in Iran are covered in dense, green forests.

Between the mountains are desert basins where little rain falls. Most Iranian towns and cities lie on these plains. The Khuzestan Plain is in southwestern Iran. Streams, canals, and rivers run through the plain and empty into the Persian Gulf. These waterways make it an ideal region for farming.

Lake Urmia, the largest lake in the Middle East, lies in northwestern Iran. Streams of water flow into Lake Urmia from the mountains, but the lake has no outlet to the sea. When the streams bring a lot of water into the lake, nearby **salt marshes** become flooded.

Minerals build up in the lake and turn its water a deep blue-green color. The water of Lake Urmia is very salty. Fish cannot survive in the lake, but many kinds of birds stop by the lake when they **migrate** in winter. Storks, spoonbills, and flamingos perch on the shores and islands.

! fun fact

Small islands and pillars of rock rise from the surface of Lake Urmia. The smallest of the 102 islands in the lake is called Osman Fist.

Persian leopard

Iran's landscapes support many kinds of wildlife. The rare Persian leopard lives in the mountains. This leopard hunts goats, sheep, wild boars, deer, and gazelle. The leopard has lost much of its **habitat** and must compete with bears, lynx, wolves, and other predators for food. Only about 1,000 Persian leopards are alive today.

wild boar

Caspian seal

golden jackal

! fun fact

The golden jackal is a kind of wild dog found in Iran. Some people think it is related to several kinds of dog breeds people keep as pets today!

The coastal waters of Iran are full of life. Dolphins and whales swim in the Persian Gulf and the Gulf of Oman. Pelicans, storks, egrets, and seagulls nest along the shores. In the north, the Caspian Sea is home to sturgeon, pike, and herring, which are hunted by the Caspian seal.

Over 76 million people live in Iran. More than half of the people are Persian. Their **ancestors** have lived in Iran for thousands of years. Azeris are the second-largest group. Gilaki and Mazandarani live along the Caspian Sea. Kurds live in the Zagros Mountains along Iran's border with Iraq. About nine out of every ten people in Iran are Muslims.

Nearly everyone in Iran speaks Persian. It is related to Old Persian, the language spoken by people who lived during the time of the Persian Empire. Some Iranians speak Azeri, Turkish, or Arabic. Many young people speak English.

Speak Persian!

Persian is written in script. However, Persian words can be written in English to help you read them out loud.

English	Persian	How to say it
hello	salam	sa-LOM
good-bye	koda hafez	KO-dah ha-FEZ
yes	bale	BAH-leh
no	na	NAH
please	lotfan	LOHT-fan
thank you	motashakkeram	MOH-ta-SHA-keram
friend	dohst	DOH-st

Did you know?

Small groups of nomads live in Iran's countryside. They move from place to place in search of grasses for their small herds of sheep and goats to eat.

bazaar

Most Iranians live in apartments in cities. They rise early on Saturday, the first day of their work week. Many people take buses to get to work. Some have cars or use motorcycles to get around. People shop at small stores or in large, open-air markets called *bazaars*.

In the countryside, homes are clustered together. People live in houses made of mud bricks or **cinder blocks**. Water is supplied from a public well. Families get up early to tend to their crops or livestock. People rest in the middle of the day when it is hottest. They return to work when it cools down.

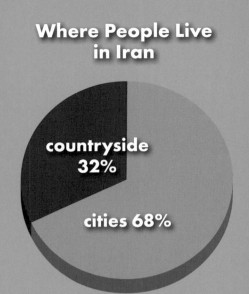

Where People Live in Iran

countryside 32%

cities 68%

Did you know?
Iran has over 5,000 miles (8,046 kilometers) of train tracks that transport people and goods throughout the country.

Going to School

In Iran, school starts with kindergarten at age 5. Students then attend elementary school from grades one through five. They study math, reading, science, Persian, and the Islamic religion. Middle school is next and includes grades six through eight. English is introduced as a second language in grade seven. Teachers assess the abilities of students and guide them toward the kind of high school they should attend. Some students attend a general studies school where they prepare for university. Others go to a **vocational school** where they train for a specific job.

In Iran, boys and girls go to separate schools. All of the teachers at a girls' school must be women, and all of the teachers at a boys' school must be men.

17

Where People Work in Iran

manufacturing 31%

farming 25%

services 44%

Did you know?

Oil is the most important natural resource in Iran. The country makes a lot of money selling its oil to other countries. Gasoline, which comes from oil, is very cheap in Iran.

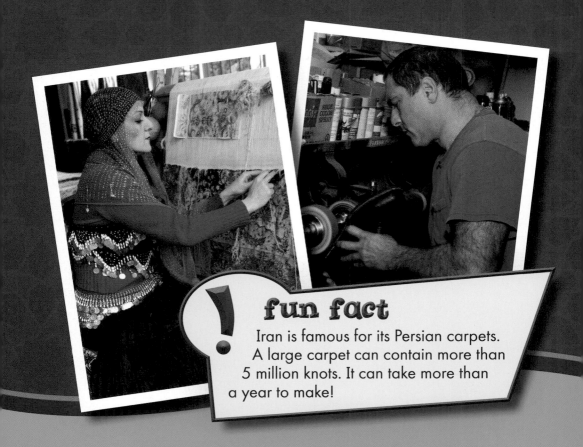

In the cities, most Iranians hold **service jobs**. They own
small shops, or they work in restaurants and hotels.
Some Iranians work in factories that make electronics,
machinery, paper, cement, and other products.

In the countryside, farmers work the land. Some raise
goats and sheep for their meat, dairy products, and wool.
Others grow wheat, sugarcane, nuts, and other crops.
Fishermen catch fish, including sturgeon, from the
Caspian Sea. Sturgeon are valued for both their meat
and their eggs, which are sold as **caviar**. Miners dig
into the earth to get copper, iron ore, and other
natural resources to send to factories in Iran's cities.

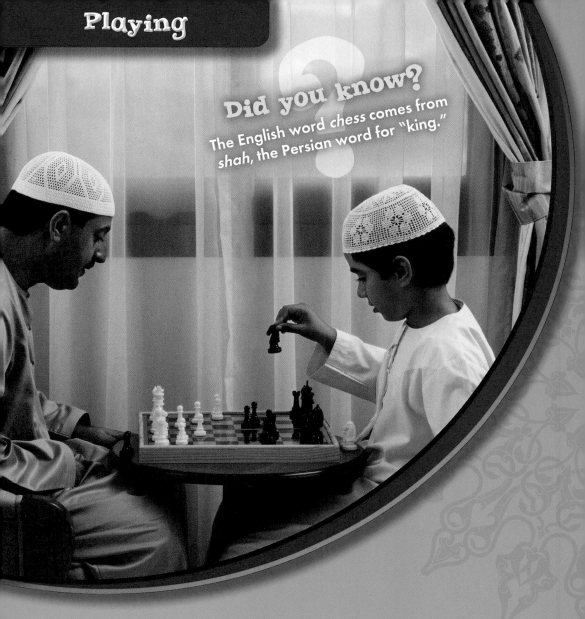

Iranians enjoy spending time with family and friends. People often meet each other at coffee shops or street markets. At cafés, friends talk and play chess or **backgammon**. In the streets and in homes, people enjoy music and talking with neighbors.

Iranians also love watching and playing sports. Wrestling is the national sport of Iran. A traditional wrestling house is called a *zurkhaneh*, or "house of strength." Wrestlers fight with heavy clubs and shields, then **grapple** in the ring. Soccer is even more popular. Children like to play it with friends after school.

fun fact

Iran's national soccer team made it to the World Cup in 2006. It has also won four gold medals at the Asian Games.

Iranians eat a variety of foods throughout the day. Breakfast usually includes bread, cheese, yogurt, fruits, and hot tea. Iranians often get lunch from small shops on the street. In the evening, people enjoy the main meal of the day. Cooks prepare lamb, chicken, fish, and beef dishes. *Chelo kebab* is the national dish of Iran. *Chelo*, or rice, is served with skewers of grilled meat called *kebabs*. Rice in Iran is often cooked with yogurt, raisins, and **saffron**. *Ash-e anar* is a popular Iranian soup made with beef, mint, peas, pomegranate juice, and other **herbs** and spices. For dessert, Iranians love *zulbia*, which are fried swirls of dough covered with honey.

ash-e anar

zulbia

chelo kebab

Iran has many national holidays. The country celebrates Revolution Day on February 11. This was the day in 1979 when the *shah*, or king, fell from power. A new government based on the laws of Islam took over the country. This made Iran an Islamic **republic**. To celebrate this event, Republic Day takes place on April 1.

Many important Islamic days are also national holidays in Iran. The Day of Ashura marks the death of Husayn ibn Ali, a Muslim **martyr** who died in battle more than 1,300 years ago. **Ramadan** is a holy month for Muslims. For Ramadan, Muslims **fast** during the day. They end the holy month with feasts and gifts.

Persepolis

Persepolis is an ancient city in southern Iran. It was built more than 2,500 years ago during the Persian Empire. In the Old Persian language, the city was called *Parsa*, which means "The City of Persians." The people who lived in Persepolis are the ancestors of many modern-day Iranians.

Ruins of the city's buildings can still be seen today. The Gate of All Nations stands on the western edge of the city. Large stone *lamassu*, or creatures with the heads of men and the bodies of bulls, still guard this gate. They welcome visitors from around the world who have come to see symbols of Iran's ancient history and culture.

Gate of All Nations

Fast Facts About Iran

Iran's Flag

The flag of Iran has three horizontal stripes. They are red, white, and green. The Arabic phrase "God is great" repeats 11 times across the bottom of the green stripe and the top of the red stripe. The national emblem of Iran appears in the center of the white band. The symbol stands for *Allah*, the word for God in the Islamic religion. Iran adopted the flag after the revolution of 1979.

Official Name: Islamic Republic of Iran

Area: 636,372 square miles (1,648,195 square kilometers); Iran is the 18th largest country in the world.

Capital City:	Tehran
Important Cities:	Mashhad, Esfahan, Tabriz, Shiraz
Population:	76,923,300 (July 2010)
Official Language:	Persian
National Holiday:	Republic Day (April 1)
Religions:	Muslim (98%), Other (2%)
Major Industries:	farming, fishing, manufacturing, mining, services
Natural Resources:	coal, natural gas, oil, uranium, iron ore, diamonds, lead, gold, opals, timber
Manufactured Products:	carpets, clothing, electronic goods, chemicals, machinery, construction materials, petroleum products, food products, metals
Farm Products:	wheat, rice, sugarcane, citrus fruits, nuts, dates, tea, dairy products, wool, caviar
Unit of Money:	rial

Glossary

ancestors—relatives who lived long ago

backgammon—a game of skill and chance played with a board, pieces known as checkers, and dice

caviar—fish eggs; Iranian caviar is famous around the world.

cinder blocks—large blocks made from concrete

dormant—not active

fast—to choose not to eat

grapple—to use the body to try to gain a physical advantage over another person

gulf—part of an ocean or sea that extends into land

habitat—the environment in which a plant or animal usually lives

herbs—plants used in cooking; most herbs are used to add flavor to food.

martyr—a person who died for his or her beliefs

Middle East—a region in northeastern Africa and southwestern Asia

migrate—to move from one place to another, often with the seasons

minerals—elements found in nature; copper, salt, and silver are examples of minerals.

natural resources—materials in the earth that are taken out and used to make products or fuel

Ramadan—the ninth month of the Islamic calendar; Ramadan is a time when Muslims fast from sunrise to sunset.

republic—a nation governed by elected leaders instead of a monarch

ruins—the physical remains of man-made structures

saffron—an expensive spice often used in Iranian food

salt marshes—flat lands that are often flooded with salt water

service jobs—jobs that perform tasks for people or businesses

vocational school—a school that trains students to do specific jobs

To Learn More

AT THE LIBRARY

Greenblatt, Miriam. *Iran*. New York, N.Y.: Children's Press, 2003.

Harris, Mark Edward. *Inside Iran*. San Francisco, Calif.: Chronicle Books, 2008.

Sheen, Barbara. *Foods of Iran*. San Diego, Calif.: KidHaven Press, 2006.

ON THE WEB

Learning more about Iran is as easy as 1, 2, 3.

1. Go to www.factsurfer.com.

2. Enter "Iran" into the search box.

3. Click the "Surf" button and you will see a list of related Web sites.

With factsurfer.com, finding more information is just a click away.

Index

activities, 20

capital (see Tehran)

Caspian Sea, 4, 5, 11, 19

daily life, 14-15

Day of Ashura, 25

education, 16-17

food, 22-23

Gate of All Nations, 26, 27

holidays, 24-25

housing, 14-15

Islam, 16, 24, 25

Lake Urmia, 8-9

landscape, 6-9

language, 12, 13, 26

location, 4-5

Middle East, 5, 8

Mount Damavand, 6

peoples, 12-13, 26

Persepolis, 26-27

Persian Empire, 4, 12, 26

Ramadan, 25

Republic Day, 24

Revolution Day, 24

sports, 21

Tehran, 4, 5

transportation, 14-15

wildlife, 8, 10-11

working, 18-19